Preparing School Counselors for English Language Learners

Luciana C. de Oliveira
Carrie A. Wachter Morris

ESOL for Different Professions Series

Typeset by Capitol Communications, LLC, Crofton, Maryland USA
and printed by Gasch Printing, LLC, Odenton, Maryland USA

TESOL Press
TESOL International Association
1925 Ballenger Avenue
Alexandria, Virginia 22314 USA
Tel 703-836-0774 • Fax 703-836-7864
www.tesol.org

Senior Manager, Publications: Myrna Jacobs
Cover Design: Tomiko Breland
Copy Editor: Tomiko Breland

TESOL Book Publications Committee

ISBN 9781942223214
Library of Congress Control Number 2015952745

Contents

Introduction

> It is frustrating for me because I know the student is struggling and needs help, and I can't do anything.
>
> Audrey, School Counselor

Like Audrey, a practicing school counselor in North Carolina, many school counselors feel they are in a frustrating situation when they think of their work with English language learners (ELLs). They know that these students may be struggling but feel at a loss without ideas or strategies to work with them. This book addresses the preparation of school counselors to work with ELLs—professionals such as Audrey who may feel they "can't do anything" when working with ELLs.

Schools that did not have an ELL population before are now seeing high numbers of ELLs among their students (Pereira & de Oliveira, 2015). Given the increase in numbers of ELLs in American schools, it is vital for education programs to address the needs of these students in their courses. *All* school professionals, including school counselors, need to be prepared to work with ELLs, not just specialist English as second language (ESL) or bilingual professionals (Paredes, 2010; Holcomb-McCoy, 2004).

This chapter examines the past and present of both the school counseling profession and ELLs in the United States. Topics included are the historical roots of school counseling, current roles and responsibilities of school counselors, legislation regarding ELLs, and an overview of knowledge that school counselors need to work with ELLs.

History of School Counseling as a Profession

Since its beginnings in the late 19th century, school counseling has changed in response to shifts in society and education. With its roots in vocational guidance, school counseling was originally a way to prepare school-aged students for employment, including helping channel students into the professions for which they were best suited. George Merrill is thought to be the originator of vocational guidance in the schools. He implemented vocational guidance in 1895 in the California School for the Mechanical Arts. In 1909, Frank Parsons, the father of vocational guidance, published *Choosing a Vocation*. He stressed that vocational guidance involved helping educate individuals about their skills, aptitudes, and strengths, teaching them about the requirements of a variety of jobs and professions, and understanding how those were related. In particular, he was concerned with educating students about the world of work, stating, "There is no part of life where the need for guidance is more emphatic than in the transition from school to work . . ." (p. 4).

From the late 1800s through World War II, school counseling and guidance was focused on vocational training. Boston schools, for example, had teachers assigned as vocational counselors in each elementary and secondary school building. These teachers were responsible for additional duties including helping students connect their academic education to the world of work, keeping track of students who were failing, urging students to complete their schooling, and maintaining occupational information (Ginn, 1924). Meanwhile, in Grand Rapids, Michigan, Jesse Davis started what is considered to be the first systematic guidance department, including teaching vocational guidance as part of the English curriculum in Grades 7–12 (Gysbers & Henderson, 2006).

While vocational guidance in schools was spreading, the way that it was implemented was not systematic, and varied from principal to principal and counselor to counselor. In 1923, Myers addressed concerns with the degree of specialization required, urging centralization, specialization, and integration into the education process. He also made another point that is still relevant to school counseling—that there is a "tendency to load the vocational counselor with so many duties foreign to the office that little real counseling can be done" (Myers, 1923, p. 141). This will be discussed further when the role of the school counselor is addressed.

During the 1920s, education shifted toward a preparation for life, more so than just preparation for college or career. Psychological measurement and testing gained in popularity and "personal adjustment" grew in prominence for school counselors. Thus, while vocational guidance remained important, it was supplemented by psychological testing and assessment and a holistic focus on students. Concurrently, personal counseling began to be seen as a separate, growing movement.

The economic hardship of the Great Depression led to a reduction in the number of school counseling positions available. This was a temporary setback, as with the onset of World War II, military testing was brought into schools. Although other roles were added, including testing aptitude and psychological traits and looking at students more holistically, linking students' education with the workplace remained a primary focus throughout this period.

Linking education with the workplace remained a primary focus until the late 1950s. With the space race that followed the launch of Sputnik came a focus on science, mathematics, and foreign language education. The National Defense Education Act (NDEA) of 1958 provided financial funding of both English as a second language and school counseling and guidance programming. It was shortly after the passage of NDEA that the term "guidance" was replaced by "pupil personnel services" (Tyler, 1960, p. 17).

During the pupil personnel services movement, counseling emerged as a central function of the school counseling profession, along with group work and consultation with parents and teachers (Gysbers & Henderson, 2006). In fact, it was recommended that between two-thirds and three-quarters of a school counselor's time was spent either counseling students or consulting with student stakeholders (Wrenn, 1962).

As school counseling continued to grow and transform, it became important to look at not just the activities of individual school counselors, but also how to establish comprehensive developmental programs. This focus took greater hold in the 1980s and 1990s, with states developing models based on their needs. A national framework for comprehensive school counseling programs was published by the American School Counselor Association (ASCA) in 2003.

Current Roles and Functions of School Counselors

School counseling has gone through a series of transformations over the years, but its current form has been defined recently by the third iteration of the ASCA National Model (2012). This model defines school counselors as members of the educational leadership team and holds them responsible for supporting the academic achievement, career development, and personal/social development of all students (ASCA, 2012). In fact, the preamble of the ASCA Ethical Standards for School Counselors states that school counselors are "certified/licensed in school counseling with unique qualifications and skills to address all students' academic, personal/social and career development needs" (2010, p. 1). In order to become a school counselor, individuals must be certified or licensed by their state department of education as a school counselor, which typically requires a master's degree in school counseling or a closely related field. Educational requirements include coursework in the following areas:

- Professional Orientation
- Human Growth and Development
- Career Counseling
- Counseling Theories
- Counseling Skills
- Group Counseling

- Social and Cultural Foundations

- Appraisal

- Research and Program Evaluation

- Supervised Field Experiences

Considering that the average student to counselor ratio for school counselors in the United States is 471:1, school counselors need to implement comprehensive school counseling programs that draw not only upon their own time and energy, but also upon resources within the school and the school community. This means collaborating with administration, faculty, staff, parents, and community organizations to ensure that student needs are met without duplicating time and efforts. It also means that school counselors need to have a working knowledge about the needs of *all students* within the school and how to help them in their academic, career, and personal/social development. When addressing the needs of ELLs, it is important that school counselors understand the diversity inherent in this population, the legislative mandates impacting ELLs, and how to help other school faculty and staff implement curricula and programs that will meet ELLs' needs.

Demographic Changes in Schools and the Need to Prepare School Counselors for English Language Learners

According to the National Clearinghouse for English Language Acquisition (NCELA; 2006), more than 10% of the K–12 student population is composed of ELLs, which represents more than 5 million students in U.S. schools. The largest number of these students is found in California, Florida, Illinois, New Mexico, New York, Puerto Rico, and Texas. However, states such as Arkansas, Alabama, Colorado, Delaware, Georgia, Indiana, Kentucky, Nebraska, North Carolina, South Carolina, Tennessee, Vermont, and Virginia have experienced more than 200% growth in the numbers of ELLs in schools from1995 to 2006 (NCELA, 2006). The numbers of ELLs have increased in all U.S. states (NCELA, 2006). The need to prepare school professionals to work with these students in all U.S. states, then, is pressing.

Legislative Decisions Affecting English Language Learners

Since the expiration of the Bilingual Education Act (BEA; 1968) in 2002, the education of language minority students has been directed by the English Language Acquisition, Language Enhancement, and Academic Achievement Act, or Title III of the No Child Left Behind Act (NCLB; 2001). In 2001, the passage of NCLB marked a new era defined by the rapid progression of the high-stakes testing movement in U.S. public education. NCLB requires states to use standardized tests to assess all students in Grades 3–8 (approximately ages 8–13) annually and once in high school. Students are categorized into subgroups if they are identified as belonging to an ethnic minority, are ELLs, have a disability, or receive free or reduced lunch. Test scores are one of the primary ways of determining if a school has made adequate yearly progress (AYP). For example, a school can be deemed "failing" because one of its subgroups did not make AYP. Schools that do not make AYP enter improvement status and are required to take a number of corrective actions. NCLB has had a great impact on the education of ELLs, like no other federal education policy since the passage of the BEA in 1968 (Menken, 2008).

Title III: Language Instruction for Limited English Proficient and Immigrant Students

NCLB provided explicit attention to ELLs. The following excerpts from Title III demonstrate some commendable intentions of NCLB (2001, SEC 3102).

> The purposes of this part [Title III] are —
>
> (1) to help ensure that children who are limited English proficient, including immigrant children and youth, attain English proficiency, develop high levels of academic attainment in English, and meet the same challenging State academic content and student academic achievement standards as all children are expected to meet;
>
> (2) to assist all limited English proficient children, including immigrant children and youth, to achieve at high levels in the core academic subjects so that those children can meet the same challenging State academic content and student academic achievement standards as all children are expected to meet, consistent with section 1111(b)(1).

The related system of accountability provides a different picture with a problematic reality for ELLs. Title III also states the following goal (NCLB, 2001, SEC 3102):

> (8) to hold State educational agencies, local educational agencies, and schools accountable for increases in English proficiency and core academic content knowledge of limited English proficient children by requiring —
>
> (A) demonstrated improvements in the English proficiency of limited English proficient children each fiscal year; and
>
> (B) adequate yearly progress for limited English proficient children, including immigrant children and youth, as described in section 1111(b)(2)(B);

One of the major problems for ELLs is that they are required to take the same exams as non-ELLs. NCLB requires states to test the English proficiency of ELLs in kindergarten through Grade 12 in listening, speaking, reading, and writing. ELLs can be granted a one-time exemption from the reading/English language arts assessment if it is their first year of enrollment in a U.S. school. However, assessment in the other content areas is still required.

ELLs can have a number of accommodations on standardized exams, including the provision of bilingual dictionaries and small group administration. States may also assess ELLs for 3 to 5 years using exams in a student's first language, if possible. In reporting, all ELLs count toward the required 95% test participation rate, but states are not required by law to include the performance of ELLs who have been enrolled in U.S. schools for less than a year. States may choose to include ELLs who have exited the subgroup by attaining English proficiency when calculating AYP for 2 years after being reclassified as fluent English proficient (Burke & de Oliveira, 2012).

The Bilingual Education Act and the *Lau v. Nichols* Ruling

The BEA signing in 1968 marked an era of support for bilingual education in the United States. Bilingual education had not been a consideration for schools serving high numbers of non-English-speaking children until 1968. Nearly all of these children were in English-only classrooms where they were left to sink or swim, as many have described it (Faltis, 2006; Menken, 2008). This act supported bilingual education and ESL programs (described later in this chapter).

The passage of BEA was followed by the Supreme Court case *Lau v. Nichols* in 1974, an extremely important case. This lawsuit was on behalf of non-English speaking Chinese students in San Francisco public schools who were placed in mainstream English-medium classrooms. The lawsuit argued that these students were not performing well in these classrooms because of their limited English proficiency. This ruling stipulated that school districts must take "'affirmative steps' to address the challenges that language poses for ELLs, by offering programs such as bilingual education or ESL" (Menken, 2008, p. 16). This case was so instrumental for the field that it is still referenced in schools in relation to programming requirements to meet the needs of ELLs (Menken, 2008). The BEA expired and was not renewed under NCLB in 2002. NCLB provides funding for the instruction of ELLs, but these programs are considerably different from those funded under the BEA. Current programs take an English-only and English immersion approach.

English-Only Initiatives

Though it is not the official language of the United States, in many contexts English often takes on that role. In recent years, this has become a topic of much heated debate which has led several states to target English-only efforts. Three significant English-only initiatives were approved in California, Arizona, and Massachusetts. In 1998, California voters approved Proposition 227 (1998), an English-only initiative targeted at the elimination of bilingual education, in a state with the largest numbers of ELLs in the country. Proposition 203 (2000) was approved by Arizona voters in 2000; this proposition limited the type of instruction available to ELLs and was passed by 63% of Arizona voters. Massachusetts voters followed and approved another state initiative, Question 2 (2002), and eliminated the oldest bilingual education law in the entire United States (Menken, 2008).

Programs for English Language Learners

There are many program types that serve ELLs in schools. The various program types are described in the next section.

K–12 English ESL: Immersion

- *ESL pull-out/English language development* (generally used in elementary school settings): ELLs spend part of the school day in a mainstream, general education classroom but get pulled out for a portion of the day to receive ESL instruction.

- *ESL push-in*: This model emphasizes keeping ELLs in the same classroom with their peers. An ESL instructor and a regular, general education teacher coteach the class and share the same classroom.

- *ESL immersion*: ELLs receive ESL instruction during a regular class period and usually receive course credit. They may be grouped for instruction according to their level of English proficiency.

- *Structured immersion*: Fluency in English is the goal. All students in the program are ELLs. There is content instruction in English with adjustments based on the proficiency level of ELLs so subject matter is comprehensible (such as sheltered English instructional methods). Typically, there is no native language support or development.

- *Submersion with primary language support*: Fluency in English is the goal. Minority language students within the majority-English language classroom (mainstream) receive help from bilingual teachers who review particular lessons covered in classes, using students' home language. This model develops very limited literacy skills in primary language.

- *The ESL resource room*: This model is a variation of the pull-out design, bringing students together from several classrooms or schools. The resource room concentrates ESL materials and staff in one location and usually has at least one full-time ESL teacher.

K–12 Bilingual Programs

- *Early-exit bilingual programs* (generally early elementary): These programs are designed to help ELLs acquire the English skills required to succeed in an English-only mainstream classroom. They provide some initial instruction in the students' home language. Instruction in the first language is phased out rapidly, with most students mainstreamed by the end of first or second grade.

- *Late-exit programs* (generally elementary): The emphasis in these programs is on developing and maintaining both ELLs' home language and English. There is a significant amount of instruction in the native language with a gradual increase of instruction in English (4–6 years).

Students continue to receive 40% or more of their instruction in their home language, even if reclassified as fluent-English-proficient.

- *Early-exit bilingual programs* (generally early elementary): These programs are designed to help ELLs acquire the English skills required to succeed in an English-only mainstream classroom. They provide some initial instruction in the students' home language. Instruction in the first language is phased out rapidly, with most students mainstreamed by the end of first or second grade.

- *Two-way bilingual programs* (also called developmental bilingual programs): The goal of these programs is to develop strong skills and proficiency in students' home language and a second language. About half the students are native speakers of English and half are ELLs from the same language group. Programs provide instruction in both languages throughout the day ("90/10": begins 90% in non-English, 10% English, gradually increasing to "50/50": 50% non-English, 50% English), they may alternate using languages morning and afternoon, or they may divide the use of the two languages by academic subject. The program may be taught by a single teacher who is proficient in both languages or by two teachers, one of whom is bilingual.

A Knowledge Base for School Counselors

Following the framework for understanding teaching and learning presented in Bransford, Darling-Hammond, and LePage (2005), we present a framework for preparing school counselors to work with ELLs (see Figure 1).

The framework has three general areas of knowledge and skills that school counselors need to develop in order to best serve the ELL population in their schools:

- **Knowledge of multicultural school counseling:** an understanding of expectations of multicultural school counseling as they apply to ELLs, counseling interventions and approaches appropriate for ELLs, and issues of language and culture in school counseling.

- **Knowledge of ELLs and second language development:** an understanding of various issues related to ELLs, such as learner characteristics and cultural understanding and second language development and pedagogical principles, including first language and second language development and linguistically responsive practices.

- **Knowledge of roles and responsibilities:** an understanding of school counselors' roles and responsibilities for the provision of direct and indirect student services to ELLs.

Each of these three areas will be addressed in the next three chapters.

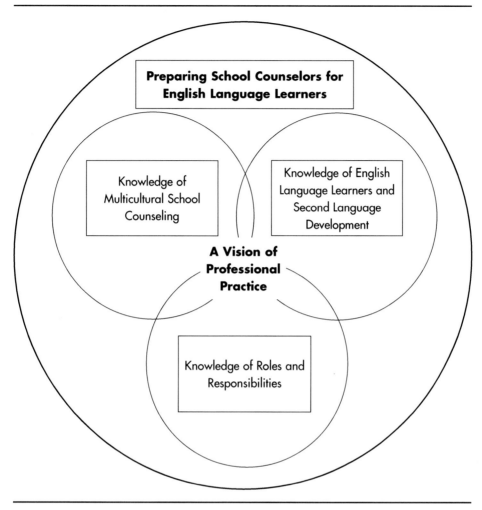

Figure 1. A Framework for Preparing School Counselors for English Language Learners

Knowledge of Multicultural School Counseling

At my school about half the population is ELL students. I feel inadequate when it comes to working with ELL students due to language barriers. My school is also one of the smallest elementary schools in my county.

Audrey, Elementary School Counselor

Like Audrey, many school counselors may feel *inadequate* in their work with ELLs because they do not have the language proficiency necessary to make connections to these students in their home languages. However, there are many ways in which school counselors can work effectively with ELLs, independent of their language proficiency in students' home languages. In the field of counseling, over the past two decades, multicultural counseling has developed as a major concept, as we explain in this chapter.

Expectations of Multicultural Counseling

Multicultural counseling has been called the "fourth force" in counseling (Pederson, 1999), a term that places it in context as one of the most influential concepts in the counseling field. School counselors serve students from every walk of life, so it is particularly important for them to understand how to work with students from diverse backgrounds. While it is challenging to be fully multiculturally competent about every cultural combination of every student in their school, school counselors need to be able to meet students where they are and work from there to help them access not only their education, but also other resources that will help them be successful in school and beyond.

Although the concept of multicultural school counseling itself is not well defined in the literature, the primary goal of multicultural school counseling is clear. It is "to prepare school counselors to integrate a critical understanding of issues relating to culture, race, social class, ethnicity, sexual identity, religious beliefs and other aspects of identity and social location into mental heath assessment and service delivery" (Ravitch, 2006, p. 18). We add to this goal the notion of *linguistic diversity*—that students who are in the process of developing English language proficiency are an important group that has often been underemphasized in the multicultural counseling literature. For the purposes of this book, we define multicultural school counseling as a call to understand the varying cultural identities and backgrounds in the schools. In order to work effectively with students, school counselors need to be able to conceptualize students, their parents/guardians, and other adults in the school within their larger contexts.

In recognition of the importance of this, school counselors graduating from a Council for Accreditation of Counseling and Related Educational Programs (CACREP) accredited master's program are required to have content in social and cultural diversity (e.g., CACREP 2001, 2009, 2016). Yet, in the CACREP 2016 standards, there is no specific mention of linguistic diversity as a concept that needs to be addressed. While it is vital for school counselors to understand the unique challenges of meeting the needs of a culturally diverse school, they can draw upon multicultural coursework and lessons about linguistic diversity to understand some of the forces that might be impacting ELLs, both positively and negatively. For example, school counselors can apply the concept of positionality to understand the way that students (both ELLs and native English speakers), teachers, families, and members of the school community define themselves and others.

Positionalities, or social locations (Robinson, 1999), are ways to understand the social value that individuals may have according to any number of viewpoints. Because positionalities "possess rank, have value, and are constructed hierarchically, particularly those that are visible and discernible" (Robinson, 1999, p. 73), there will be some aspects of an individual's cultural identity or position that may be valued or privileged. Other aspects of a cultural identity may be oppressed. So, for example, in traditional American culture, a White heterosexual woman from a lower socioeconomic background has both privileged (e.g., White, heterosexual) statuses and oppressed (female, more impoverished) statuses. Individuals have multiple positionalities that form a constellation of privilege and oppression that shape how individuals views themselves, those they come into contact with, and the world around them.

Using this concept of positionalities to understand an individual's context can help school counselors understand how the different contexts of a student's identity may be affecting him or her, both inside and outside of school. Although language status is just one of many different cultural identities that each student has, it is incredibly important—particularly if a student's English fluency and receptive language are in initial stages of development and if the school does not have easily accessible resources developed for the student's native language. With the importance of education as a vehicle for economic and social success, students who are unable to fully engage with their education due to a language difference are disadvantaged in accessing that education. We urge readers to remember, however, that ELLs also may have specific strengths that could provide resilience and help connect the school to the community.

In order to provide culturally responsive services to every student, school counselors need to develop their understanding about culture. Culture has been defined as a way of life and the "context within which we exist, think, feel, and relate to others" (Brown, 2007, p. 188). It is important to mention that culture can be depicted in an oversimplified manner, which may lead to generalizations and stereotypical characterizations of individuals who have similar cultural backgrounds. Stereotypes develop when group characteristics are ascribed to individuals simply based on their cultural backgrounds (Brown, 2007).

Dimensions of Culture and the Process of Acculturation

When talking about culture, some English language teaching scholars have referred to "big C" and "little c" culture. Big C—Culture—is often used to refer to contributions such as architecture, literature, and music, while little c—culture—refers to our everyday lives (Murray & Christison, 2011). Culture has also been referred to as a process and not content (Kramsh, 1998). Murray and Christison (2011), drawing on Levy (2007), describe a framework that can help professionals understand the contexts in which they work. Figure 2 represents the five key dimensions of the framework.

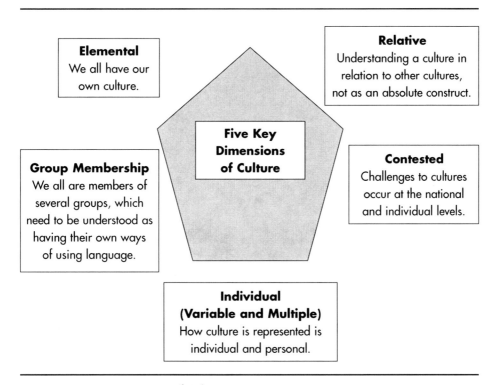

Figure 2. Five Key Dimensions of Culture

These five key dimensions can help school counselors consider the influence of culture in their consultations with any student. Each of these dimensions of culture is explained in the figure. *Culture as elemental* refers to how each person has their own culture but may be unaware of our cultural beliefs and understandings. *Culture as relative* refers to the aspect of culture that is only understood in relation to other cultures. *Culture as group membership* is the side of culture involving multiple memberships in a variety of groups in society. *Culture as contested* refers to the challenges to culture at national and individual levels. Finally, *culture as individual (variable and multiple)* refers to the representation of culture as individual and personal. In Chapter 3, we apply these dimensions specifically to working with ELLs and their families.

Another aspect of cultural learning that is broadly applicable is the process of acculturation. Acculturation has been referred to as the development of a new cultural identity. Acculturation is a complex process that can disrupt a person's self-identity and ways of being. If it does, this may lead to culture shock, which may involve a wide range of feelings and psychological crisis. Culture shock has been described as the second out of four stages of culture acquisition (Brown, 2007). The four stages of additional culture acquisition are described in Figure 3.

Stage 1 is excitement and euphoria, where everything in the new culture is fresh and exciting. Stage 2 is culture shock, where there is frustration with differences and feelings of anger, unhappiness, and homesickness. Stage 3 is gradual recovery, where individuals begin to accept the differences between their culture

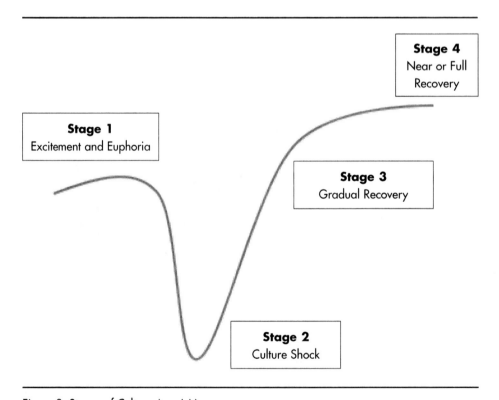

Figure 3. Stages of Culture Acquisition

and the new culture and start to understand the second culture. Stage 4 represents near or full recovery, either assimilation or adaptation, where individuals understand many aspects of the new culture and accept it more fully. Broad application of the process of acculturation and adaptation to ELLs is discussed further in Chapter 3.

Multicultural Competencies

The Association for Multicultural Counseling and Development (AMCD) constructed a set of multicultural competencies that provides a nice baseline for multicultural competence. In discussing multicultural competence, Ratts et al. (2015) provide a discussion of the specific competencies that "culturally skilled" counselors need to have. These multicultural competencies include the ability to: 1) maintain awareness of personal assumptions, values, and biases; 2) empathetically understand the worldview of people from diverse backgrounds and maintain a general understanding of multicultural issues; and 3) develop and use appropriate interventions, strategies, and techniques for a multicultural and diverse population. While this document provides valuable information and guidance for working with the range of students that a school counselor will serve in the schools, it does not always account for the resources and requirements of a school setting. Holcomb-McCoy (2004) tailored the multicultural competencies to be more applicable to school counselors in her School Counselor Multicultural Competencies Checklist, which is duplicated below. When reading through this checklist, take note of your reactions to your own personal areas of competence and challenge.

School Counselor Multicultural Competence Checklist (Holcomb-McCoy, 2004, pp. 184–186)

Multicultural Counseling

1. I can recognize when my attitudes, beliefs, and values are interfering with providing the best services to my students.

2. I can identify the cultural bases of my communication style.

3. I can discuss how culture affects the help-seeking behaviors of students.

4. I can describe the degree to which a counseling approach is culturally inappropriate for a specific student.

5. I use culturally appropriate interventions and counseling approaches (e.g., indigenous practices) with students.

6. I can list at least three barriers that prevent ethnic minority students from using counseling services.

7. I can anticipate when my helping style is inappropriate for a culturally different student.

8. I can give examples of how stereotypical beliefs about culturally different persons impact the counseling relationship.

Multicultural Consultation

9. I am aware of how culture affects traditional models of consultation.

10. I can discuss at least one model of multicultural consultation.

11. I recognize when racial and cultural issues are impacting the consultation process.

12. I can identify when the race and/or culture of the client is a problem for the consultee.

13. I discuss issues related to race/ethnicity/culture during the consultation process, when applicable.

Understanding Racism and Student Resistance

14. I can define and discuss White privilege.

15. I can discuss how I (if European American/White) am privileged based on my race.

16. I can identify racist aspects of educational institutions.

17. I can define and discuss prejudice.

18. I recognize and challenge colleagues about discrimination and discriminatory practices in schools.

19. I can define and discuss racism and its impact on the counseling process.

20. I can help students determine whether a problem stems from racism or biases in others.

21. I understand the relationship between student resistance and racism.

22. I include topics related to race and racism in my classroom guidance units.

Understanding Racial and/or Ethnic Identity Development

23. I am able to discuss at least two theories of racial and/or ethnic identity development.

24. I use racial/ethnic identity development theories to understand my students' problems and concerns.

25. I have assessed my own racial/ethnic development in order to enhance my counseling.

Multicultural Assessment

26. I can discuss the potential bias of two assessment instruments frequently used in the schools.

27. I can evaluate instruments that may be biased against certain groups of students.

28. I am able to use test information appropriately with culturally diverse parents.

29. I view myself as an advocate for fair testing and the appropriate use of testing of children from diverse backgrounds.

30. I can identify whether or not the assessment process is culturally sensitive.

31. I can discuss how the identification of the assessment process might be biased against minority populations.

Multicultural Family Counseling

32. I can discuss family counseling from a cultural/ethnic perspective.

33. I can discuss at least two ethnic group's [sic] traditional gender role expectations and rituals.

34. I anticipate when my helping style is inappropriate for an ethnically different parent or guardian.

35. I can discuss culturally diverse methods of parenting and discipline.

Social Advocacy

36. I am knowledgeable of the psychological and societal issues that affect the development of ethnic minority students.

37. When counseling, I consider the psychological and societal issues that affect the development of ethnic minority students.

38. I work with families and community members in order to reintegrate them with the school.

39. I can define "social change agent."

40. I perceive myself as being a "social change agent."

41. I can discuss what it means to take an "activist counseling" approach.

42. I intervene with students at the individual and systemic levels.

43. I can discuss how factors such as poverty and powerlessness have influenced the current conditions of at least two ethnic groups.

Developing School-Family-Community Partnerships

44. I have developed a school-family-community partnership team or some similar type of group that consists of community members, parents, and school personnel.

45. I am aware of community resources that are available for students and their families.

46. I work with community leaders and other resources in the community to assist with student (and family) concerns.

Understanding Cross-Cultural Interpersonal Interactions

47. I am able to discuss interaction patterns that might influence ethnic minority students' perceptions of inclusion in the school community.

48. I solicit feedback from students regarding my interactions with them.

49. I verbally communicate my acceptance of culturally different students.

50. I nonverbally communicate my acceptance of culturally different students.

51. I am mindful of the manner in which I speak and the emotional tone of my interactions with culturally diverse students.

Reflections on School Counselor Multicultural Competence Checklist

Upon reading through this checklist, what were your thoughts? Which areas did you feel were overall strengths of yours? How might you use those strengths to improve the climate of your school? Conversely, which are areas that you identified as areas for further growth for yourself? Of those, select the two biggest priorities for further development. What are ways that you could increase your level of competence in those two areas?

We encourage school counselors to think broadly about culture and how it is relevant to all students in their schools. In the next chapter, we apply these concepts more specifically to the ELL population.

Knowledge of English Language Learners and Second Language Development

3

> Our ELL teachers work with [ELLs] more and discuss various issues and then bring me in. My ELL population [is] the faithful parents who come to ... event[s]; however, I don't think our events are as language friendly towards them as they should be.
>
> Lucy, School Counselor

ELL teachers, as Lucy highlights, have many responsibilities in working with ELLs, and they often seek school counselors' assistance. We know that school counselors can have an even more significant impact in ELLs' lives if they develop their knowledge about ELLs and second language development, which this chapter addresses. We start out by providing some important information about ELLs and their families, learner characteristics, and cultural understandings.

Knowledge of English Language Learners

ELLs are not a homogeneous population of students. They can be newcomers to the United States or have been born and lived all of their lives in the country. ELLs may be children of immigrants or international students. Immigrants are newcomers who typically intend to live permanently in the U.S. They can be naturalized citizens, permanent residents, refugees, asylum visa holders, or undocumented. International students typically come for a short period of time for study or work and intend to return home. ELLs' parents or guardians may or may not speak English, so it is important to know whether school counselors would be able to use English with them or if translation services will be needed during the consultation process. As described by Lucy in the chapter opening quote, ELL parents go to school events and often care a lot about their children's academic success, contrary to some beliefs.

Many ELLs have been born in the United States and have always attended U.S. schools. These students do not often have the opportunity to develop literacy skills in their home languages, and therefore may not read or write in their home languages. ELLs who were not born in the United States, but immigrated at an early age, may have limited or no literacy skills. However, if ELLs came to the United States in late childhood or as adolescents, they very likely will have developed their literacy skills in their home languages, unless they had interrupted schooling in their home countries. These students, often called students with interrupted formal education (SIFEs), are usually refugees, newcomers who had no choice but to leave their home country and begin a new life in a new country. The challenges for all ELLs to learn English will highly depend on their experiences with schooling in their home countries and whether or not they developed their literacy skills in their home languages.

Some questions about ELLs that school counselors need to ask are:

1. Who are the ELLs you are counseling?

2. What are their ethnic and linguistic backgrounds?

3. What are their home languages?

4. What are their educational experiences in their home countries (if not born in the United States)

5. What are their life experiences?

The five key dimensions of culture and the process of acculturation addressed in Chapter 2 are highly relevant both when conceptualizing ELLs and when deciding how to work with them and their families in the school context. Attending to these can help school counselors consider the influence of culture in their consultations with ELLs and their families.

As ELLs learn English, they are also learning culture. Second language learning involves the development of a second identity along with a second language (Brown, 2007; Téllez & Waxman, 2006). And while the process of acculturation and adaptation is relevant to any individual who is learning a new culture, the process is complex and may not occur the same way for ELLs as it would for a student in a similar situation who is a native speaker of English.

As was described above, ELLs are not a homogeneous population of students. All of their contextual differences play a role in how ELLs view the new culture. For example, students who have immigrated with their families may face competing pressure to assimilate to mainstream American culture while also maintaining their cultural identities from their former country. How this process is navigated differs from individual to individual and family to family. It also takes time. Anticipating culture shock and helping normalize both the challenges and benefits of coming from a different country can be helpful for ELLs who have immigrated. Students who immigrated prior to adolescence may also find themselves having to adjust to challenges unique to what is known as being a 1.5 generation immigrant: The identity of these immigrants is split, and they may not identify either with their home culture and the culture of their parents or with American culture.

While going through the acculturation process, ELLs may experience psychological blocks and may feel alienation in the process of learning a new language and developing more knowledge of the new culture. This alienation can be from their own home culture, the new culture, and from themselves as individuals (Brown, 2007). School counselors need to know that ELLs may be experiencing different feelings of frustration or anxiety in the new culture that may exhibit themselves in a variety of forms both inside and outside of the school environment. For this reason, it is important that school counselors look at each ELL holistically, rather than focusing solely on language development. This frustration and anxiety may impact not only personal/social development, but also academic achievement and career development.

Knowledge of Second Language Development

Language learning involves three aspects: learning language, learning through language, and learning about language (Halliday, 1993). Students who are learning English as first language or a second language are *learning language*. All teachers are responsible for developing their students' language abilities. Teaching any content area involves teaching the vocabulary and organizational structures common to that content area. Students also *learn through language* because they are in classrooms where language is used all of the time. Students listen to lectures, read textbooks and other course material, talk about content, write papers. They use language in everything they do in classrooms. They also *learn about language*, or learn about how language works. They may learn about grammatical aspects of language and how different texts are used in different subjects in school.

First Language Development

Children develop the capacity to comprehend language and to produce and use words to communicate. From birth, children are exposed to their first languages and develop their capacity to successfully use language. Children cannot develop their language abilities without social interactions. There is a typical developmental sequence that children's language development follows (see Table 1), but variation in the age at which children reach a given landmark is common.

Most researchers agree that children are able to develop their first languages without formal language instruction. This topic is a lot more controversial when it comes to the development of second languages. We have been using the term "language development" because we believe in the social nature of language. However, the literature differentiates *acquisition* and *learning*. *Acquisition* refers to a process in which children acquire language naturally while *learning* refers to a more conscious process which helps children attend to different aspects of language.

Table 1. Typical Sequence for Children's Language Development (based on Menyuk & Brisk, 2005)

Stage	Typical age
Babbling	6–8 months
One-word stage	9–18 months
Two-word stage	18–24 months
Telegraphic stage or early multiword stage	24–30 months
Later multiword stage	30+ months

Second Language Development

The first language acquisition process is very important for ELLs. ELLs' first—or home—language has an important role in second language development. ELLs develop a second language by drawing on their background experiences in their first language. When ELLs have a strong foundation in their first language, the process of second language development involves language transfer. Language transfer refers to the transfer of forms and meanings as ELLs use their productive skills (i.e., speaking or writing) in the second language. Language facilitation is referred to as positive transfer when there are similarities in the two languages. Language interference occurs when differences between the first and second language cause a nonproductive transfer. For example, learners may use features of their first language in experimentation with the second language. This reliance on the first language serves to help ELLs construct an *interlanguage*, a transitional system that has a structurally intermediate status between the first and second languages (Selinker, 1972).

Stages of Second Language Development

When learning English, ELLs move through five predictable stages: Preproduction, Early Production, Speech Emergence, Intermediate Fluency, and Advanced Fluency. ELLs' movement through the stages depends on many factors, including educational background, first language experiences, and length of time spent in the country.

Stage I: Preproduction

Often called the silent period, ELLs are starting to develop their English language proficiency and may have receptive abilities (listening and reading), but they are in the process of developing their productive abilities (speaking and writing). ELLs listen attentively and may be able to respond to visuals, including pictures. They may be able to answer yes/no questions by pointing and can understand and use gestures and body movements to show comprehension. At this stage, ELLs need repetition of English words, phrases, and sentences.

Stage II: Early production

At this stage, ELLs can usually speak in one- or two-word phrases and use short language chunks that have been memorized. They can answer yes/no and either/

or questions by using one- or two-word responses. They are typically able to participate in some whole class activities and best learn vocabulary if supported by pictures. They are able to learn more about writing through labeling and short sentences.

Stage III: Speech emergence

ELLs at this stage can communicate with simple phrases and sentences. They can ask simple questions and initiate short conversations with classmates. They are able to understand stories read in class with the support of pictures and are able to do most classroom work with teacher support. Graphic organizers and other visual support are particularly helpful at this stage. Learners typically understand teacher explanations and simple directions.

Stage IV: Intermediate fluency

At this stage, ELLs use more complex sentences and use both receptive and productive skills. They ask questions about classroom materials and typically are able to work in grade-level content areas. ELL writing at this stage will have many errors as students are developing their ability to use English grammar and sentence structure. They are better able to understand complex concepts.

Stage V: Advanced fluency

ELLs are able to function in class and perform in content-area learning as well as other fluent English proficient students. Most ELLs at this stage have been exited from ESL and other support programs. Some errors of convention may still appear in writing.

It is more than likely that ELLs in schools will be at a variety of stages in the second language development process. These different stages of second language development were used to develop the different levels of language proficiency commonly used to describe ELLs. These levels of language proficiency, presented in Table 2, are very important for everyone involved in the education of ELLs to know.

Linguistically Responsive School Counselors

In addition to understanding the stages of second language development and language proficiency, school counselors need to develop certain orientations and skills in order to work with ELLs and their teachers in their planning for instruction that is linguistically responsive and differentiated according to the language level of ELLs. The next section explains these orientations and skills, based on a framework for preparing linguistically responsive teachers developed to prepare mainstream teachers for ELLs (Lucas, Villegas, & Freeedson-Gonzalez, 2008; Lucas & Villegas, 2010, 2011). This evolving framework draws on conceptions of culturally responsive teaching (e.g., Villegas & Lucas, 2007) and the related literature on the preparation of mainstream teachers for ELLs (e.g., de Jong & Harper, 2005, 2008; Schleppegrell, 2004; Fillmore & Snow, 2005), and can be used to inform what school counselors need to know about ELLs.

Table 2. English Language Proficiency Levels

Level	Language Performance Expectations
	English language learners:
Level 1 (Starting)	• can respond to some simple communication tasks. • can use language to communicate around basic needs.
Level 2 (Emerging)	• respond to more varied communication tasks. • use high frequency and common vocabulary words and expressions in oral or written short sentences, but often with errors that impede communication.
Level 3 (Developing)	• adapt their English language skills to meet their immediate communication and learning needs. • use more general and specialized vocabulary and syntax. • communicate with others on familiar matters and to understand and be understood in many basic social situations. • exhibit many errors of convention that may impede the communication but retain much of its meaning.
Level 4 (Expanding)	• are able to use English in concrete and abstract situations as a means for learning in the academic areas, although some minor errors of conventions that do not impede the communication may still be present. • understand and use specialized academic vocabulary and expressions and construct sentences with varying linguistic complexity and lengths in oral and written communication.
Level 5 (Bridging)	• communicate effectively with various audiences and recognize implicit meanings. • speak, understand, read, write, and comprehend in English without difficulty and use technical academic vocabulary and expressions. • use sentences with varying linguistic complexity and lengths in extended oral and written communication. • use oral and written language that is comparable to their English-proficient peers.

Note. Adapted from Teachers of English to Speakers of Other Languages. (2006). *PreK–12 English language proficiency standards* (p. 39). Alexandria, VA: Author.

Essential Orientation and Skills

Sociolinguistic Consciousness
This element highlights that one's way of using language is influenced by and closely linked with sociocultural and sociopolitical factors, including race, ethnicity, social class, and identity. School counselors need to understand the connection between language, culture, and identity and to develop an awareness of the sociopolitical dimensions of language use and language education. They understand that it is neither effective nor ethical to expect ELLs to learn English at the expense of leaving behind their home languages and dialects.

Value for Linguistic Diversity
Linguistically responsive school counselors show their respect for and interest in diverse students' home languages. Such positive attitudes toward students' home

languages send caring and welcoming messages that encourage students' engagement in school learning.

Inclination to Advocate for ELLs

Linguistically responsive school counselors actively address the learning of ELLs and work to improve one or more aspects of ELLs' educational experiences (Athanases & de Oliveira, 2011). ELLs differ immensely in culture and language from English-speaking school personnel; this can create a barrier that hinders communication at school, which in turn poses an obstacle to building a connection between school personnel and students. Advocating for greater equity is especially important for ELLs, who tend to be marginalized and invisible in the school context.

Learning About ELLs' Language Backgrounds, Experiences, and Proficiencies

Because of the fundamental role played by what a learner brings to learning, it is essential that school counselors understand ELLs' diverse language backgrounds, experiences, and proficiencies. Counselors need that understanding to be able to tailor their counseling to take into account ELLs' resources and needs.

Identifying the Language Demands of Potential Classes

Because access to learning in school requires facility with the language of school, linguistically responsive school counselors must be knowledgeable about the academic language and literacy demands of the potential classes in which ELLs could enroll. ELLs' learning from mainstream classroom discourse (e.g., the specific linguistic forms, functions, and vocabulary) is highly dependent on the kinds of experiences they have in classes. School counselors assist students in selecting their classes so their educational experiences are positive. Therefore, a school counselor's ability to facilitate this process is influenced by his or her knowledge of the language demands of the potential classes in which ELLs can enroll.

Applying Key Principles of Second Language Learning

Linguistically responsive school counselors understand the process through which ELLs develop English proficiency while they are also learning various content areas. Key principles of second language learning include:

1. Conversational language proficiency is fundamentally different from academic language proficiency.

2. ELLs need comprehensible input just beyond their current level of competence.

3. Social interaction for authentic communicative purposes fosters ELL learning.

4. Skills and concepts learned in the first language transfer to the second language.

5. Anxiety about performing in a second language can interfere with learning. (Lucas & Villegas, 2011, p. 65)

Additional ELL-Focused Competencies for School Counselors

While we find the Association for Multicultural Counseling and Development Multicultural Competencies (Arredondo et al., 1996) and the School Counseling Multicultural Competencies Checklist (Holcomb-McCoy, 2004) that were presented in Chapter 2 provide valuable information and guidance for dealing with the range of students that a school counselor will serve in the schools, the former does not always account for the resources and requirements of a school setting and the latter does not attend to the specific needs of linguistically diverse students and families. In order to direct attention to the specific needs of linguistically diverse students in a school setting, we have provided additional competencies. School counselors:

- understand different linguistically-appropriate counseling approaches that can be used with ELLs with different English language proficiency levels.

- are aware of their stereotypical beliefs regarding language background and how those might impact the counselor/client relationship.

- know how linguistic considerations play into consultation.

- are able to recognize linguistic issues and how they might impact the consultation process.

- have specific knowledge about facilitating conversation about different aspects of linguistic diversity with a variety of stakeholders.

- are knowledgeable about the sociocultural influences on linguistically diverse student populations.

- are aware of community resources to support ELLs and their families.

- understand interaction patterns that might influence ELLs' thoughts of integration.

- are aware of the manner in which they speak to ELLs and are able to adjust their language in order to better reach these students.

This chapter described what school counselors need to know about ELLs and second language development. We provided some important information about ELLs and their families, learner characteristics, and cultural understandings. We then explored issues in second language development, including the stages of language development and the different levels of language proficiency. Finally, we looked at the essential orientations and skills of linguistically responsive school counselors. In the next chapter, we look at the roles and responsibilities of school counselors in their work with ELLs.

Knowledge of Roles and Responsibilities

I usually meet with [ELLs] and their families when they first enroll and introduce them to the ELL teacher, and we come up with a course plan that will work best for them and their English skills at the time. I continue to meet with them throughout the semester to make sure things are going as planned and communicate with parents as needed and make necessary changes to the course plan.

Brittany, School Counselor

School counselors, like Brittany, have many roles and responsibilities in working with all students. This chapter addresses what school counselors need to know about their roles and responsibilities for the provision of direct and indirect student services to ELLs. We start out by providing an overview of the American School Counselor Association (ASCA; 2003, 2005, 2012) National Model and discuss how the model applies to working with ELLs.

Roles and Responsibilities of School Counselors

School counselors are responsible for the academic, career, and personal/social development of all students under their care (ASCA, 2012). In order to best meet the varied needs of students, school counselors develop comprehensive school counseling programs that utilize varied methods of delivery of direct and indirect services to students. One of the primary models for implementation of comprehensive school counseling programs is the ASCA (2003, 2005, 2012) National Model, visually depicted in Figure 4.

Figure 4 presents four primary elements of the ASCA National Model: Foundation, Delivery System, Management System, and Accountability. The Foundation describes what the school counseling program is and includes the competencies that each student should reach as a result of a comprehensive

Figure 4. The ASCA National Model. Reprinted with permission from American School Counselor Association. (2012). *The ASCA national model: A framework for school counseling programs* (3rd ed.). Alexandria, VA: Author.

school counseling program. The Delivery System addresses the methods through which the comprehensive school counseling program is implemented. These methods typically include classroom guidance, individual and small group counseling, responsive services to meet immediate needs, and the systems support that is required to establish and grow the school counseling program. The Management System addresses the stakeholders involved in the development of the school counseling program, the use of data to support and evaluate the program, and action plans that define how the comprehensive school counseling program will be delivered to all students. Finally, the fourth element is the Accountability System. This system addresses how students and the school community are different because of the school counseling program. It includes performance evaluations of the school counselor, data reports, and formative and summative evaluations of different aspects of the school counseling program.

In addition to the four elements of the ASCA National Model, four themes underscore the model. These themes—leadership, advocacy, collaboration and teaming, and systemic change—are core values and are related to the roles of a school counselor attending to the National Model. Indeed, they address ways in which school counselors can effect systemic change through effective leadership in the school system, student-centered advocacy, and collaborative teaming with school staff, students, families, and the larger community. This systemic change is aimed at minimizing or eliminating barriers to student success.

Although the ASCA National Model serves to describe the ideal comprehensive school counseling program, it does not dictate exactly how each aspect of the model would look from school to school. Decisions on specific programming and how a comprehensive school counseling program is implemented fall directly to a school's counselors and to the administrative team that supports those counselors. Thus, programs can appear quite different from school to school, depending on the specific needs and supports available to the school and its surrounding community. In order to help guide school counselors in best practices for working with all students within their school, ASCA has also crafted ethical standards (2010) to guide daily practice and position statements related to certain parts of the job, including everything from corporal punishment to working with sexual minority students. Related specifically to working with ELLs, there is a position statement on cultural diversity that was originally established in 1988 and revised most recently in 2009.

This position statement on cultural diversity notes that

> Professional school counselors are expected to "specifically address the needs of every student, particularly students of culturally diverse, low social-economic status, and other underserved or underperforming populations" (ASCA, 2005, p. 77) . . . [and] collaborate with stakeholders to create a school climate that welcomes and appreciates the strengths and gifts of culturally diverse students. Professional school counselors act as advocates for those who are marginalized by working with systems to address inequities in schools (Holcomb-McCoy, 2007). (ASCA, 2009, p. 1)

Additionally, the position statement outlines that a school counselor's role in cultural diversity includes

> creating a school climate where cultural diversity is celebrated; curriculum, textbooks, pedagogy, and classroom management methods are inclusive; and cultural relations within the school are encouraged and embraced. . . . School counselors also seek to enhance their own cultural competence, and facilitate the cultural awareness, knowledge, and skills of all school personnel. (ASCA, 2009, p. 1)

Thus, this position statement calls for school counselors to take action to ensure students of culturally diverse backgrounds have access to appropriate services and opportunities promoting the individual's maximum development (ASCA, 2009, p. 1). Others addressing the role of school counselors with ELLs have noted that school counselors are vital for ELL dropout prevention (McCall-Perez, 2000). The preamble of the ASCA ethical standards mentions language, immigration status, and ethnic/racial identity specifically when it states that "each person has the right to be respected, be treated with dignity, and have access to a comprehensive school counseling program that advocates for and affirms all students from diverse populations" (ASCA, 2010, p. 1), going so far as to state that "special care [should be] given to students who have historically not received adequate educational services, e.g., students of color, students living at a low socio-economic status, students with disabilities and students from non-dominant language backgrounds" (p. 1).

ASCA, the dominant professional association for school counselors, and other researchers (e.g., McCall-Perez, 2000; Paredes, 2010) have spoken directly of the benefits of school counselor support for ELL populations. Yet, school counselors often receive little information about how to work with ELLs. In fact, a search of the 2009 Council for Accreditation of Counseling and Related Educational Programs (CACREP) Standards revealed language mentioned three times, none of which were specific to ELLs, and rather stressing that a school counselor "understands the effects of . . . language . . . on student learning and development" (SC A.6, p. 39), "[d]esigns and implements prevention and inter-vention plans related to the effects of . . . language . . . on student learning and development" (SC D.3, p. 40), and "[a]ssesses and interprets students' strengths and needs, recognizing uniqueness in cultures, languages, values, backgrounds, and abilities" (SC H.1, p. 42). The 2016 CACREP Standards, however, do not mention language specifically, opting for terminology that is more general and broadly related to sociocultural diversity.

Although there is a rapidly expanding ELL population and a call for school counselors to serve the needs of all students, including ELLs, there may be limited opportunity for formal and informal professional development about how school counselors can best serve ELLs. Even with the challenges of receiving professional development, school counselors who recognize that they might have a skill gap around meeting the needs of ELLs can advocate for increased train-ing, or take opportunities like independent reading and study to help inform them. Appendix A includes a variety of resources, including research articles, best practices articles, and websites that school counselors can use to increase their awareness and knowledge of how to work with ELLs in their schools. The remainder of this chapter discusses ways that school counselors can work with ELLs and school stakeholders through provision of direct and indirect student services. Specific vignettes and case studies highlight areas where school coun-selors may need to reflect on their ethical standards and work within the school culture to reduce or remove systemic barriers that could detract from ELLs' ability to be successful.

School Counselor Roles With English Language Learners

School counselors serve many roles with students in their schools. In order to better conceptualize how school counselors work with ELLs, we begin by explor-ing the roles of the school counselor that underpin the ASCA National Model.

School counselors are charged with meeting the academic, career, and personal/social development needs of all students in the school. As the themes underscoring the ASCA National Model (2012) attest, in order to best serve ELLs, school counselors act as advocates, leaders, collaborators, and agents of systemic change. These roles are foundational to school counselor training, thus, the application of them to ELLs should work in concert with the skills and foci that school counselors already have in their schools. These roles blend together in ways that make effective school counselors pivotal in connecting ELLs, their families, and the community to the school, which is then enriched for their presence.

School Counselor as Advocate and Agent of Systemic Change

School counselors may need to advocate for ELLs to help them gain access to the resources that support their success in the school environment. Included in this advocacy is school-level leadership in identification of structural and systemic barriers to ELL success as well as building targeted supports for ELLs and other students. In order to do this, school counselors must work collaboratively both within the school and in the outside community, to build school-family-community partnerships that will support communication and student-based learning. Through these actions, the school counselor acts as an agent of systemic change, reducing or eliminating barriers to student success and increasing student supports and cross-cultural understanding.

Specific to school-level advocacy efforts, schools may have limited staff with the language fluency or cultural knowledge to transition new students into the school and support their continued growth and development. For example, school counselors may need to advocate for infrastructure supports and appropriate in-service activities to help faculty and staff understand best practices for working with ELLs and their families. School counselors have a unique perspective of the school because of their contact with students and their focus on creating a comprehensive school counseling program that supports the educational mission of the school and the development of all students. Given this perspective, school counselors must take an active leadership role in examining the needs of the ELL population and then advocate for changes that can be made in the school environment.

In order to identify areas where targeted advocacy efforts may be most needed, school counselors can conduct needs assessments examining access to services and identifying curricular delivery or communication gaps. Once the needs of the ELL population are determined, a school counselor can serve as an advocate for the ELL population at the school. This may include recommending hiring or retaining new personnel (e.g., ESL teacher or coordinator, translators, or academic paraprofessionals), identifying communication gaps in school information delivery systems that need to be addressed (e.g., translations of websites or materials into languages represented within the community, gauging whether information may need to be available in both print and audio format to communicate with those who may not be literate in their dominant language), or finding ways to help those from the dominant culture understand the cultural beliefs and contexts of ELLs within the school.

School counselors can also use data from needs assessments to identify areas where in-service training might be helpful for school faculty and staff. Taking a leadership role in preparing and delivering relevant in-school services may help school faculty and staff focus on topics relevant to ELLs, including helping the school community gain cultural knowledge or awareness regarding the backgrounds of the ELLs within the school population, increasing faculty and staff's ability to communicate or teach in ways that support learning content knowledge and the English language, or supporting student learning about each other's cultural backgrounds and increasing receptivity to diversity in the school.

In situations where resources may be scarce and funding may not be available, locating alternative sources of funding (e.g., grants, private funders) or tapping into community expertise and stakeholders to provide resources may also be necessary. School counselors can take a leadership role in the identification of funding, writing grant or foundation proposals, or making contacts within the business community to secure supports for increasing resources for ELLs. Even if funding from outside sources is not available, school counselors can advocate, lead, and collaborate within their school and district to form school-family-community partnerships to better connect the school with key stakeholders in the community. This can be particularly helpful and relevant for ELLs.

School Counselor as Leader and Collaborator

In working with ELLs and, indeed, immigrant populations in general, it is particularly important to use collaborative skills to build school-family-community partnerships (see, e.g., Dotson-Blake, Foster, & Gressard, 2009). "School – family – community partnerships have been shown to meet the diverse needs of students, enhancing student success by fostering connections among the people who play central roles in children's lives" (Dotson-Blake et al., 2009, p. 234). Dotson-Blake, Foster, and Gressard discuss a model for how to develop school-family-community partnerships focused on Mexican-American immigrants, but we would argue that a similar model could be used to connect with families and communities composed of individuals from a variety of ethnic and linguistic backgrounds. The model presented by Dotson-Blake et al. consists of six steps:

1) Foster respect and culture of equal engagement

2) Create a welcoming, collaborative climate

3) Identify cultural brokers and community leaders

4) Plan intentional, structured opportunities to interact

5) Bolster investment through community engagement and reciprocity

6) Reflect on the success and effectiveness of partnership efforts (Dotson-Blake et al., 2009, p. 235)

By engaging with families of ELLs and creating connections between the school and key community leaders, the school counselor demystifies the school for parents of ELLs, and creates a school environment in which families and the community at large feel supported and represented. Benefits of this sort of partnership include increased parent involvement; clearer expectations and communication among parents, the school, and the community; and the ability to involve community leaders in the school so that they act not only as role models for the students but also as key components of the school communication network. A school-family-community partnership can also help school counselors identify ways to reduce stressors related to acculturation or cultural conflict between ELLs and their parents.

School Counselor as Cultural Broker

An additional role of school counselors that we find particularly important is that of a cultural broker. In her research, Paredes (2010) proposed that school counselors play a role as a cultural broker with ELLs, ". . . help[ing] ELLs convert their already-held skills . . . into usable skills . . . in the school environment" (p. 40). The role of cultural broker is often described as one held by an individual who can translate languages. When looking at school counselors as cultural brokers, Paredes (2010), however, references the role they play helping ELLs, non-ELLs, their families, and the school community understand and exchange their cultural capital. This role of cultural broker is consistent with the values undergirding the ASCA National Model, where a school counselor serves as an advocate, a leader, a collaborator, and an agent of systemic change.

Examples of Services Provided by School Counselors for ELLs

Through consistently evaluating the school environment and the community regarding its supports and barriers to ELLs' success, school counselors can continue to build resources and infrastructure to support ELL learning, while honoring their students' families, their cultural identity, and the communities in which they live. These activities, run concurrently with ongoing staff training and increased awareness of the needs of ELLs, help school counselors take on the role of systemic change agent, while also allowing them to model for other school personnel, families, and students ways to be supportive of each other. While the individual needs of each school and community may vary, the following three examples are typical services that may be implemented at any school working with an ELL population. We highly encourage school counselors working with ELLs to perform a needs assessment specific to the needs of both the school and the ELL community it serves in order to identify additional points of contact that support ELL students and their families.

Conduct a Formal Orientation for ELLs

All ELLs and their families can benefit from a specialized orientation conducted in a manner that helps them feel connected to and supported by the school. Whether the ELL students are recent immigrants or have lived in the United States since birth, presenting information on the education process in place for

ELLs in the school as well as providing attention to the specific services in the school and community for ELLs will give students and families a shared understanding of the expectations and the supports in place for students.

If the school serves ELLs who are newcomers to the United States, school counselors can provide a part of the orientation that would explain the various expectations of the school, its functions, and various issues related to being a student in their new country. If possible, the school counselor could investigate the ELLs' cultures and incorporate comparisons of the educational environment ELLs are coming from to the one they are entering. This would allow for ELLs, their families, and the school staff to identify and understand some of the ways in which the new school and life environment may be culturally different in ways beyond the language difference. Examples of important cultural differences may be time spent in school, time management, class times, and procedures for changing classrooms. For example, in some countries (e.g., Brazil), secondary school teachers are the ones who change classrooms during a particular school day and students remain in their own classrooms, just as at the elementary school level in the United States.

Conduct a Professional Development Session About Working With ELLs

In a complementary manner to the orientation process, school counselors can conduct an orientation for school personnel working with ELLs as professional development for their school. This professional development session could be to explain strategies for working productively with ELLs, tips for engaging with ELLs' families, cultural differences related to school expectations for the ELL populations served, as well as ways that school counseling services can be utilized effectively by the school faculty and staff to support ELLs. If a school counselor recognizes the need for this type of professional development, but also identifies that he or she needs more information in order to create it, looking to local civic or educational resources to provide support may be a way to enlist help to provide needed professional development for both the school counselor and the rest of the school faculty and staff.

Administer Language Proficiency Tests

School counselors are often responsible for administering language proficiency tests to determine the level of English language proficiency of ELLs. These tests are then used to determine the appropriate placement of ELLs in classrooms as well as the language support they need to receive in order to support their success in school. It is important for school counselors to know about the high stakes nature of these language proficiency tests for ELLs, which will help determine the kinds of language services that ELLs receive during the school year.

Responsibilities of School Counselors
With English Language Learners

While school counselors provide a variety of activities to students, the school, and the community at large, these activities are often broken into two primary categories: direct student services and indirect student services. In the next sections of this chapter, we discuss these two types of services and offer case studies and questions to prompt thoughtful reflection on how school counselors can offer services that would support ELLs in the situations presented.

Direct Student Services

Direct student services refer to all aspects of a school counseling program that are provided specifically to students without an intermediary (ASCA, 2012). In most cases, these activities are delivered through individual counseling, small group counseling, and classroom guidance activities. Direct student services are supposed to compose 80% of school counselor time (ASCA, 2012).

The ASCA National Model (2012) refers to three broader categories of direct student services: school counseling core curriculum, individual student planning, and responsive services. School counseling core curriculum includes delivery of content and skill-development for all students in the school. This curriculum is typically implemented in a structured way, and it often involves collaboration with a number of stakeholders, rather than individual lesson plans presented by the school counselor on each topic. Individual student planning refers to working with students to set and attain goals and develop plans for their future. This might involve 4-year planning for high school students, postsecondary planning, and individual meetings with students to do academic or career planning. Responsive services are intervention-focused (rather than prevention-oriented) activities and designed to meet immediate needs. Examples of responsive services include crisis response and personal/social counseling in individual or small group settings.

The content covered by these three categories of direct student services may overlap and include (but are not limited to) academic planning, career development, crisis response, personal/social support, delivery of prevention-based information, and psychoeducational lessons. Thus, rather than discussing the broader categories, we will focus on the traditional vehicles of direct student service delivery: individual counseling, small group counseling, and classroom guidance.

Individual Counseling

Individual counseling refers to a school counselor working one-on-one with a student on issues related to academic, career, or personal/social development. In working individually with ELLs, particularly those who are Level 1 (starting) or Level 2 (emerging) students, school counselors would ideally have access to a trained translator who can not only help translate the content of an individual session but also understands and is held to similar limits of confidentiality. Unfortunately, whether due to budget limitations or limited access to translators of a specific language, use of a trained translator may not be possible.

Additionally, even with a trained translator, there may be nuances in what is being communicated (see Hamerdinger & Karlin, 2003).

While cultivating translation resources and advocating for translation needs may help school counselors plan for anticipated events (e.g., scheduled postsecondary planning), even those with some access to translation services may not be able to access them at every instance needed. Thus, it is especially important to remember that school counselors are not limited to talk-based therapy. Different modalities including sandplay therapy, art therapy, play therapy, and other creative interventions may be used in lieu of or as supplements to traditional talk-based therapy for all students, but particularly for ELLs.

One area where many school counselors working with middle and high school ELLs may face challenges is in 4-year planning for ELLs—particularly those with more limited English proficiency. In states that have a variety of high school diploma tracks, it is the authors' experience that students with limited English proficiency have, at times, been automatically placed in the least academically challenging diploma track, with minimal consideration to alternative options or educating the student about the limitations that diploma track might have on postsecondary educational options. Individual contact with students around scheduling and course registration, while deemed a noncounseling task by ASCA, remains an area where many school counselors, particularly at the high school level, spend an inordinate amount of time. This is certainly not an ideal activity, but it does allow for the ability to touch base with each student individually to discuss academic needs and postsecondary planning. While it is important for school counselors to coconstruct 4-year plans that will allow students to graduate, it is equally important that those plans are reflective of the academic abilities of the student. By working with classroom teachers to understand the academic capabilities and progress on academic English skills for each student, school counselors may be able to coconstruct 4-year plans with ELLs that allow both for postsecondary education opportunities and the ability to graduate on time if progress made on academic English is slower than anticipated.

When working individually with ELLs, a school counselor who does not have any fluency in the student's native language can keep in mind a few key strategies to help ease communication. These strategies can be useful in individual work with students, but would also apply in small group and classroom guidance settings. Some examples of these strategies include:

- Speak clearly so that ELLs can try to understand (speaking louder will not help ELLs understand better)

- Pause often

- Use hand gestures and body language to support meaning

- Repeat key points

- Paraphrase when possible

- Use synonyms

- Avoid the use of idioms and other phrasal expressions that may be difficult for ELLs

- Use examples when possible

These are further explained in Table 3, which delineates other strategies appropriate for classroom instruction.

Small Group Counseling

Small group counseling would include school counselors meeting with a handful of students to help those students relate to and learn from each other as well as the counselor. Small groups may be focused on a specific topic (e.g., divorce, building friendship skills, grief and loss) or be more general and prevention-oriented in nature. ELLs may benefit from small groups in a number of ways, depending on their specific needs. For example, if several ELLs transfer into a school midyear and are having trouble meeting people or fitting into the school community, a school counselor might arrange a small group consisting of the ELLs and a few of their carefully selected classmates to help forge connections with their peers in the school community. This same small group could also serve to help native-English speakers understand the key strategies for communication listed above.

Classroom Guidance

Classroom guidance activities often take place in previously-established classes or homerooms. During classroom guidance, a school counselor may help a teacher address an ongoing issue in his or her class (e.g., appreciation of diversity, informing about cyber safety), present on a topic that needs to reach a large number of students (e.g., information about PSATs or SATs, dissemination of a school-wide character education curriculum), or work with a teacher to augment curriculum (e.g., meeting with an English class to discuss themes like depression or bullying that have emerged in young adult literature assigned for the class).

Table 3 provides some strategies for teachers that school counselors can use in their work in the classroom setting.

Now that we have discussed the ways that school counselors can help serve ELLs through direct services, it is time to apply what we have discussed to a case study. Case studies can help school counselors prepare for and consider issues they have yet to come across in their own work, or think about how they might have handled a situation in the past differently. In the following case example, consider the issues for ELLs to help guide your reflection and response about the situation described. Finally, examine multiple sides to the problems and apply those to situations beyond this particular example.

Case Study 1: Direct Services

Cale is a first-year school counselor in a large rural high school. He is one of five counselors serving a student body of 2,300 students. One of the tasks he is about to undertake for the first time is creating 4-year plans. During each spring semester, each of the school counselors is responsible for completing a 4-year

Table 3. Strategies Used by Linguistically Responsive Teachers

Strategy	Examples
1. Build language-rich environments	• Provide ELLs with opportunities to listen, read, speak, and write in English • Provide ELLs with opportunities to develop advanced language proficiency
2. Pay attention to language	• Speak clearly—enunciate • Use steps in giving directions and repeat key points • Paraphrase • Pause often
3. Modify, don't simplify, instruction	• Modify *how* you present information to students, not *what* you present • Present challenging content • Ask questions when you present information • Model the expected performance
4. Provide opportunities for ELLs to communicate with other students	• Plan activities where ELLs can interact with fluent peers • Provide role models of language (including bilingual fluent peers) • Plan heterogeneous groups
5. Create various opportunities for ELLs to understand and process the material	• Plan for teacher-directed instruction • Include individual, pair, and group activities • Arrange textbook reading (with or without teacher help)
6. Use multimodal strategies	• Use oral and written language • Use visual (e.g., pictures, flash cards, graphs, manipulatives) and auditory (e.g, video, music) materials • Use direct experience (field trips, walks around school) • Use nonverbal communication (body movements and expressions)
7. Identify the language demands in texts you assign	• Identify what is challenging in the texts you assign—beyond vocabulary! • Identify the background knowledge ELLs need • Discuss how textbooks are organized
8. Establish language and content objectives	• Consider what you expect ELLs to learn about language and content
9. Scaffold ELLs' academic language and content learning	• Involve ELLs in all classroom activities • Provide temporary assistance so that ELLs are able to complete a task on their own
10. Make connections to students' language(s) and culture(s)	• Use examples that are relevant to students' culture(s) • Use students' home language(s) as a resource in the classroom

Note: Adapted from Pereira, N., & de Oliveira, L. C. (2015). Meeting the linguistic needs of gifted English language learners: What teachers need to know. *Teaching Exceptional Children, 47*(1), 208–215.

plan with every ninth-grade student and auditing the 4-year plans for 10th-, 11th-, and 12th-grade students. These 4-year plans map out the courses that students will take during high school and are vital for ensuring that students meet graduation requirements. Cale understands that his state has multiple diploma types, each of which is tailored to meet different postsecondary goals. For example, students hoping to attend a 4-year college are required to take more rigorous math and science courses and will have to have, at minimum, 2 years of a foreign language. Thus, the diploma type that college-going students would map to in their 4-year plan has different requirements than the diploma that is focused more on meeting basic high school standards and preparing students to go directly into the workforce or enlisting in the military. So, while the more academically rigorous diploma types open up a range of postsecondary options, the less academically challenging diploma types might mean that students might have to pursue additional coursework after graduation to meet minimal requirements for postsecondary education.

Although he understands that just having any sort of high school diploma is preferable to having a student drop out, Cale is hopeful that he can engage with each of his ninth-grade students at a level that encourages them to consider the more rigorous diploma types. He experiences some success in his first dozen meetings, and gains confidence in his approach. The next student he sees is Sabir, a level 1 (starting) ELL from Bengal. Immediately, Cale realizes that he and Sabir are having difficulty communicating about the 4-year plan. Not only is there a language difference, but Sabir also lacks the cultural understanding of postsecondary education and training opportunities, and how decisions made might impact his future. At a loss for what to do, Cale quickly gets the attention of a more experienced school counseling colleague.

As his colleague gets started, Cale notices that she deftly steers Sabir towards the least challenging diploma—one that requires a four-course sequence of "career-oriented" coursework. She asks if Sabir likes art, and he nods, although Cale is not sure whether Sabir really understood the question. In about 5 minutes, Sabir's 4-year plan is complete with a career sequence in art and the minimum possible credits in math, science, social studies, and English. ESL courses are also in the 4-year plan, and there is plenty of elective and study hall space on the plan "so that he'll have room to retake the courses he's going to fail."

As his colleague hands Sabir a pass back to class and whizzes back to her office, Cale feels unsettled about what looked like an automatic decision to track Sabir to the minimum standards for a high school diploma without even considering what Sabir's interests, strengths, and talents might be.

Reflection Questions

1. What are your thoughts about the situation described above? If you were in that situation, what would be your initial response? How would you personally balance the dilemma facing Cale?

2. Generate a list of potential options for the student. What would you advise the student to do?

3. In an ideal situation, (e.g., if there were no time, personnel, or financial limitations), how might this scenario be changed?

4. How might other types of direct services be utilized to support 4-year planning with all students, but particularly ELLs?

Reflection on Case Study 1

This situation is not atypical, and it has a lot of complexity, particularly for school counselors in schools or districts that struggle with 4-year graduation rates and burgeoning student populations who speak languages different from the languages of school counselors, faculty, and staff in the school. Without easy access to a translator, many of these conversations must happen in spite of a significant language difference. Given these challenges, there are several options that Cale might have in working with ELLs with limited to no English fluency.

Option 1: Place students in classes in which he is confident they will be able to succeed, even if those classes potentially short-circuit a student's ability to pursue postsecondary education.

Option 2: Place students in a variety of courses that would allow for a balance of challenge and ease, and allow for at least two diploma types, depending on language acquisition and performance throughout high school.

Option 3: Place students in a challenging curriculum, while also attempting to build in support resources (e.g., access to tutoring and translation services) as appropriate and hope that the student rises to the challenge.

Option 4: Allow students to make the choice, regardless of ability to communicate understanding of potential challenges or limitations implicit in the choice made.

Each particular case has complexity based on individual students' contexts, so we are not going to lay out a "best option" for fear of it becoming prescriptive for all situations. Rather, we urge professional school counselors to consider the full background and potential of each student, including consideration of skills and assets that might help them succeed. When possible, mapping at least two options and trajectories that allow for growth as well as helping meet the basic diploma requirements can help students gain a high school diploma, but also the potential to develop more complex academic skills and pursue postsecondary education or vocational training options after high school.

Indirect Student Services

While direct student services include interaction between school counselors and students, indirect student services include activities performed to benefit students but that involve interaction between school counselors and individuals other than the identified students (e.g., parents, teachers, community resources, staff). Indirect student services should compose approximately 20% of school counselors' time. Typically, indirect student services fall into three primary categories: referrals, consultation, and collaboration.

Referrals

School counselors refer students to outside resources for a variety of academic, career, and personal/social concerns that are either beyond the scope of the school counselor's expertise or require more extensive time than a school counselor can provide in the context of the school day. For example, academic referrals may be to outside tutors or academic support agencies. A student looking for additional information for college might be referred to a university admissions or financial aid office. A student struggling with depression or having thoughts of suicide might be referred to a local community mental health provider. A family struggling with food insecurity or with paying for electricity or heating bills might be referred to community support systems.

It is a school counselor's responsibility to be knowledgeable about the wide range of agencies and supports that could benefit students. Specific to working with ELLs, school counselors may want to be sure to keep track of a variety of resources and events including the following:

- Translation services in a variety of languages

- Library services (e.g., bilingual events, adult ESL or literacy support)

- Cultural centers

- Local college or regional university services (e.g., admissions help, FAFSA days)

- Support services for undocumented students and families

Consultation

School counselors work directly with teachers, parents, and other stakeholders to support student learning and development. Consultation can take place in many forms, including working with teachers to identify barriers to student learning, working with parents and school staff to promote consistency between messages delivered at home and at school, and working with other mental health and education professionals to support student transitions. Particularly for students who have recently moved from another country, significant time might be spent in consultation with staff from a student's country of origin and with teachers at the new school to help a student integrate into the school as smoothly as possible.

Collaboration

Similar to consultation, collaboration involves school counselors working with identified individuals or entities. Defined as "a style of direct interaction between at least two coequal parties voluntarily engaged in sharing decision making as they work toward a common goal" (Friend & Cook, 1992, p. 5), collaboration helps school counselors and other stakeholders in students' lives and students' education to think through ways to support student growth and development. The ASCA National Model suggests that collaboration can take multiple forms, through teaming and partnering, school/district committees, and parent workshops (2013). We would add that regardless of the form or the venue, the key to collaboration is making sure that the individuals at the table look at shared goals or specific student outcomes and think through strategic ways that they can each contribute to removing obstacles or providing supports that help students meet those targets. One specific way that collaboration can be used to support ELLs is to identify families, members of the business community, and other key community stakeholders, including those that share the cultural and linguistic backgrounds of ELLs, and involve them in the process of supporting ELLs at the school. Whether that be through helping with program development, translation services, providing personnel or resources to support programming, or helping increase school/community partnerships, collaboration is a valuable skill set for all school counselors, but it is particularly vital for those working with ELLs.

Case Study 2: Indirect Services

As with the section of the chapter on direct services, we now turn to application through a case study. Reflect on the following situations, and imagine that it is this person's job as the school counselor to figure out how to address, through collaboration and consultation, how welcoming and supportive the school is for not only new families, but also a growing population of ELLs. Lisa is the school counselor in an elementary school of about 450 students. The scenarios described below are a few brief interactions that Lisa has observed in her day-to-day activities in the school. How would Lisa, through indirect services, work to establish an environment that will help ELLs successfully join the school community?

Scenario 1: "Put your coat on. It's cold outside"

As Lisa walks down the hallway during a cold day in late October, she notices several kindergarten students getting ready to go outside for a field trip. She also notices one of the kindergarten teachers speaking loudly with an ELL, Hasan, saying, "Put your coat on. It's cold outside." Hasan, a Level 1 (starting) Arabic speaker, looks lost and just stares at the teacher without knowing what to do. Mrs. Smith, the teacher, increases her voice considerably as she notices Hasan does not understand what she said; still Hasan does not move. The teacher continuously repeats the same command, "Put your coat on. It's cold outside," but Hasan at this point is almost crying and still does not move.

Scenario 2: Level 2 ELL Not Engaged in
Mainstream Third-Grade Classroom

Mrs. Dixon, a third-grade teacher, comes to Lisa and tells her that a Level 2 (emerging) ELL, Jean, is not engaged in classroom activities and often looks lost when the teacher is reading a storybook or doing other in-class activities. Other students try to get Jean involved and often ask him to participate, but he doesn't seem to want to. Sometimes he will cry and say that he does not want to do anything. The teacher tells Lisa that she has tried to reach his parents but has had no luck getting a call back from them.

Scenario 3: Low ELL Parental Involvement in Schools

Both Mrs. Dixon and Mrs. Smith tell Lisa that they have seen very low ELL parental involvement in school, with very few parents of ELLs signing up for classroom volunteer activities. They and other teachers feel frustrated because they keep providing opportunities to volunteer. The ESL teacher, Mr. Lewis, tells the teachers that he has noticed that parents are motivated to be involved but just do not know what to do because they are unfamiliar with the school culture. Teachers do not know what to do to increase parental involvement.

Reflection Questions

1. What are some of the issues at play in these three scenarios?

2. As a school counselor, how could Lisa help the teacher(s) in these particular situations?

3. How could Lisa work with the teachers, parents, and other school personnel through collaboration and consultation? Give concrete examples of actions she could take.

4. What roles can school counselors play in similar situations?

5. How can school counselors be ELL advocates without undermining teacher authority?

Reflection on Case Study 2

Scenario 1: "Put your coat on. It's cold outside"

In the first scenario, we see a teacher who is not communicating nonverbally with the ELL and is not using body language or gestures, likely because of time constraints, and an ELL who likely thinks he is doing something wrong and is nervous or scared about it. The role of the school counselor in this instance can be one of consultant and collaborator. One alternative in this situation would be for Lisa to ask the teacher "would you mind if I helped Hasan put his jacket on?" Then, if the teacher says yes, Lisa could model the use of nonverbal cues, gestures, and body language and show exactly the action that the student needs to take. At a different time, so that the teacher doesn't feel undermined in front of students, Lisa could ask to speak with the teacher and mention her difficulties in communicating with ELLs. Then the school counselor can provide some ideas for ways to work with ELLs to help them in and beyond the classroom.

Scenario 2: Level 2 ELL Not Engaged in Mainstream Third-Grade Classroom

In the second scenario, the ELL is not engaged and we do not really know why. A school counselor's role in this situation may be to gather information about things happening both within and outside the school to try to understand the Jean's larger context and see what factors might be impacting him in school. For example, Jean's family may be working through issues regarding food scarcity or a family loss. If he is a refuge, Jean may have a previously experienced trauma that could be contributing to his behavior. Another possibility is that there is something specific to the school environment that is increasing Jean's discomfort. Through a combination of direct services (e.g., individual counseling with Jean) and indirect services (e.g., consultation with Jean's teachers and other relevant adults in the school, observation of Jean at mealtimes or recess, consultation with Jean's parents or guardians), Lisa can work to identify factors that might be negatively impacting Jean and also identify ways that Jean could be better supported in the school. Once ways of reducing barriers and increasing supports are identified, the school counselor can help school faculty and staff implement them as appropriate in the school setting.

Scenario 3: Low ELL Parental Involvement in Schools
The third scenario highlights a disconnect between the school and home cultures. This disconnect may be contributing to a teacher misconception about parental involvement. The ESL teacher is working to change the misconception, but it may be difficult to change without increased involvement from ELL parents and guardians, and the existing gulf between teachers and ELL parents seems to be widening.

Lisa's role in this scenario would be to work to identify barriers to family involvement in the school. This may occur through a needs assessment of parents, working with the ESL teacher or members of the ELL community to understand their cultural norms around educational involvement for parents and guardians, and helping ELLs and their families feel like valued members of the school community. For some parents and guardians, work schedules may conflict with the typical opportunities available for parents to volunteer. For others, transportation to the school site may be limited or unavailable. Still others may have childcare needs that do not allow for them to take full advantage of the opportunity to volunteer in the school. Lisa, working in concert with others, can work to identify ways to expand opportunities for the families of ELLs (and all students) to engage with the school community. Once barriers are identified, soliciting parent involvement and helping build the connection between parents, teachers, and the school can help ELLs' families feel like welcomed and valued members of the school community.

This chapter described the roles and responsibilities of school counselors in their work with ELLs. Through using a variety of direct and indirect services, school counselors are leaders and advocates in the school for all students. By using their collaborative skills, school counselors can work for systemic change that supports ELLs and their families in the school and the community. In the final chapter, we bring attention back to the framework for preparing school counselors for English language learners (Chapter 1, Figure 1) and discuss implications for school counselors' next steps in working with ELLs.

Final Application and Conclusion

School counselors are responsible for the academic, career, and personal/social development of all students in their schools (ASCA, 2012). Because of the burgeoning population of ELLs in schools, it is vital that school counselors know how to reach and support this specific student population. Yet traditionally, information about how to best work with ELLs, their families, and the community around ELL-related issues may not be adequately integrated into school counselor preparation programs. Therefore, school counselors may graduate with a general understanding about multicultural school counseling, but not with enough content in their programs to fully prepare them for their work with ELLs. Our goal with this book was to address this gap. We framed the book around a knowledge base for school counselors for working with ELLs and organized it to present a conceptual framework that helped organize information relevant to school counseling of ELLs. In this chapter, we revisit Figure 1 (Chapter 1), "a framework for preparing school counselors for English language learners."

Developing School Counselors' Knowledge Base for Working With ELLs

To recap, the framework has three general areas of knowledge and skills that school counselors need to develop in order to best serve the ELL population in their schools (see p. 15):

- Knowledge of multicultural school counseling

- Knowledge of English language learners and second language development

- Knowledge of roles and responsibilities

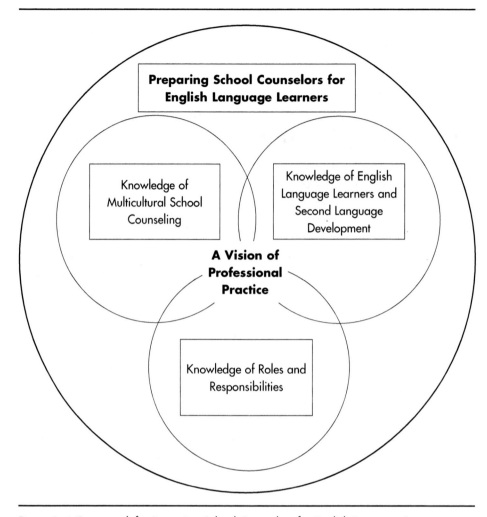

Figure 1. A Framework for Preparing School Counselors for English Language Learners

Chapters 2, 3, and 4 provided information about each of these three areas. We learned that in order to transform the school setting into a more equitable environment for ELLs, school counselors have to work with other school professionals. Well-prepared school counselors are in an ideal position to assist ELLs through direct and indirect services. Professional school counselors may inform and guide colleagues about essential knowledge related to ELLs as well as provide guidance and content that leads to specialized educational services for these students.

Final Case Study Application

Now that we have discussed the many roles and responsibilities of school counselors, along with the ways that they can help serve ELLs, it is time to apply what we have discussed to a final case study. In the following case example, consider the issues for ELLs to help guide your reflection and response about the situation described. Finally, examine multiple sides to the problems and apply those to situations beyond this particular example.

Case Study 3, based on a real classroom situation, depicts a mainstream classroom. In this particular classroom, ELLs are divided up into the first-grade mainstream classrooms, regardless of language of origin or presence of a learning disability. As you read Case Study 3, consider some of the variables at play here. Try to imagine yourself serving the role of the school counselor, who was observing the classroom at the time the incident in the case study occurred, to help provide insight into how to support ELLs' learning and development in the school. What in this classroom supports student learning and development? What negatively impacts student learning and development? In your role as the only school counselor in the school, how might you implement programming that would support the learning and development of ELLs in this classroom?

Case Study 3: Mainstream First-Grade Class

Mrs. Reeves has eight ELLs in her classroom. There are three Level 3 (developing), two Level 2 (emerging), and two Level 1 (starting) Spanish speakers, and there is one Level 3 Korean speaker. The two Level 1 students speak no English at all; however, one of these students is able to pick up on hand gestures and other nonverbal cues. The other student, Maria, cannot understand even simple hand gestures and will only speak in Spanish. Maria often cries because she thinks she is getting in trouble, or she doesn't want to do what the teacher has asked of her. In addition to the language barrier, the teacher believes she also has some type of learning disability that has not yet been identified. There is a teacher's aide that comes to the class when Mrs. Reeves needs her. The aide will speak Spanish with the student to try to figure out the problem, but she says that this student is very hard to understand even in her native language, which would suggest that she has problems speaking Spanish.

The teacher teaches a Korean class after school sometimes, so she has many resources in this language. The Korean student in the class is about a Level 3, so she knows and speaks English pretty well. The teacher will talk to her in Korean, clarify directions, and give her worksheets written in Korean. At times, the teacher also writes the words of books in Korean underneath the ones in English. The teacher does not do this for any of the other students. In fact, all of the Spanish speakers are often in the back of the room and typically receive very little attention from the teacher. Mrs. Reeves has told the teacher's aide that the Spanish speakers are too difficult to handle and this may be due to their illegal immigrant status in this country.

Reflection Questions

1. What are some of the issues at play in this case study?

2. What problems do you see in this classroom?

3. How is the teacher including ELLs in the classroom environment? How could she work with ELLs differently?

4. What about Maria, who may potentially also have a learning difference? What can the teacher do to support this ELL in the classroom? What can you do as a school counselor to assist in the identification process?

5. Imagine that you are the school counselor and have been asked to work with Maria on sociocultural issues and developing more comfort in the school and classroom setting. What sort of direct services might be particularly beneficial to her? How would you deliver those services if you had access to a translator? How would you deliver them if you did not have access to a translator?

6. Imagine the teacher's aide came to talk with you about what she feels is problematic treatment of the Spanish speakers in this classroom. What are some issues you could discuss with the teacher? How would you support the various stakeholders in this situation: the teacher, the ELLs, and the teacher's aide? What sort of direct services might be appropriate for the students in this classroom (including Spanish-speaking ELLs, and native-English speakers)?

Reflection on Case Study 3

There are many complex factors at play in this case study. We see preferential treatment for the Korean student by the teacher that appears to result from both a similar language background or cultural understanding and some negative perceptions of the Spanish-speaking students. There is a clear bias exhibited by the teacher against the Spanish-speaking ELLs who, therefore, are not given the same opportunities as the other students in the classroom. As with any group of neglected and segregated students, the Spanish speakers may engage in disruptive behavior because they are disengaged with the rest of the classroom. In such a situation, it would be easy for the teacher to simply blame them for their disciplinary problems rather than see her own contribution to their behavior.

For Maria, if there is the possibility that there might be some sort of learning difference, the school counselor can help work with the classroom teacher to begin the response to intervention (RtI) process to determine whether the difficulties she has exhibited are due to language differences, underlying learning differences, or a combination of the both. Collaboration among appropriate personnel in the school or district to initiate this process will help Maria's learning difference be identified early, and she can start receiving support, if warranted. In some school districts, this may be difficult as there may be misconceptions that conflate ELL status with having a learning difference when the issue may solely be due to the language difference. Sometimes, it may be difficult to separate language-related challenges in school from specific learning differences that could be identified through RtI, allowing students to receive needed special education support.

Regardless of the situation, school counselors would need to work with the teachers and Maria, and advocate for Maria if there is evidence that she is struggling in multiple areas in ways that go beyond what would be expected from a language development standpoint. For example, if Maria is also struggling in ESL, or in areas where she is able to communicate in Spanish, that is important to note for any potential testing or identification purposes.

It is vital to form a relationship with Maria, through an appropriate direct services method. Ideally, a combination of individual counseling, supported by either small group or classroom guidance, can give a school counselor insight into not only how Maria functions on her own, but also with others. These activities would ideally be done with access to a translator, but if none is available, the school counselor can use other resources, such as pictures or toys, to give Maria visual cues to support accurate communication.

It is also important to make contact with Maria's parents or guardians, regardless of her progress through the RtI system. Not only is it mandated as part of the identification process (should one be needed), but it is best practice to include parental involvement when possible. Enlisting parental help not only builds trust but also can give school counselors further information about how Maria behaves in the home environment.

If involving Maria in small group counseling, the school counselor could use a group as a vehicle to help her interact with her peers. The school counselor can have a key role in helping Maria make friends, which would make her feel more comfortable and less anxious. Another option to assist Maria in connecting to the school is to have her work with the school counselor for a few days, doing some language-light jobs in different parts of the school in hopes to build her confidence.

With the teacher's aide, it is important for the school counselor to demonstrate that he or she is there to assist by getting to know the exact concerns, the expectations, and the possible outcomes. Then the school counselor can discuss how he or she could either come into the classroom and assist or help address the concerns. These concerns can begin to be addressed by talking with the teacher and the teacher's aide to show that the classroom would be a better place to learn for all students if all are involved in the schooling process. The teacher needs to know that some students are being left out, and learning is not taking place for those students. Some useful strategies could be discussed for making the classroom a more cohesive learning atmosphere. This would mean ensuring that the Spanish-speaking ELLs are involved in classroom activities. It is important to frame this discussion and any suggestions so that they are not punitive; the counselor's language should convey that he or she understands the specific classroom context and wishes to help problem solve. It is also important to show the teacher, very candidly, that there are many misconceptions about ELLs as being "illegal" when in fact they may have been born in the United States and, therefore, are U.S. citizens (as described in Chapter 3). These misconceptions about immigration status need to be demystified for the entire school personnel. More important, it must be made clear that schools have the obligation to serve all students, regardless of their immigration situation.

As professionals with specialized preparation, school counselors are in an ideal position to have an impact on ELLs' futures by serving as student advocates and facilitating significant changes for these students in schools. As presented in Chapter 3, school counselors' skills can help them identify strategies to work in and beyond the classroom to support ELLs and assist teachers in their work with ELLs.

Recommendations for School Counselor Educators

While school counseling programs have required courses that focus on multi-cultural school counseling, language diversity may not be specifically addressed. If covered at all, it may be embedded within diversity-related topics to give context (e.g., language diversity might be briefly addressed with a unit on Latino/Hispanic ethnicity). We urge school counselor educators to recognize that language diversity is a complex area of sociocultural diversity in and of itself, and to ensure that all counselors—and specifically school counselors—receive at least a basic level of knowledge and training in understanding language diversity. It is important for future school counselors to be prepared to work with ELLs to address their needs.

We also understand that programs may have full curricula already, and may not have as much room as they would like to address the myriad challenges and populations that school counselors will work with in practice. Thus, we also recommend that in curricula about ethical codes and professional orientation, as well as the supervision of field experiences, school counselor educators and supervisors remind school counselors-in-training about the need to address recognized gaps in training and expertise through ongoing professional development and clinical supervision, both pre- and in-service. Being aware of community resources and experts who can help school counselors connect to this issue or learn how to build their own network provides good modeling for lifelong learning and allows school counselors-in-training to learn how to continue to build expertise that is critical in schools. Appendix A provides some resources for professional development.

References

American School Counselor Association. (2003). *The ASCA national model: A framework for school counseling programs* (1st ed.). Alexandria, VA: Author.

American School Counselor Association. (2005). *The ASCA national model: A framework for school counseling programs* (2nd ed.). Alexandria, VA: Author.

American School Counselor Association. (2009). The professional school counselor and cultural diversity. Retrieved from https://www.schoolcounselor.org/asca/media/asca/home/position%20statements/PS_CulturalDiversity.pdf

American School Counselor Association. (2010). Ethical standards for school counselors. Retrieved from http://www.schoolcounselor.org/files/EthicalStandards2010.pdf

American School Counselor Association. (2012). *The ASCA national model: A framework for school counseling programs* (3rd ed.). Alexandria, VA: Author.

Arizona Secretary of State. (2000). *Proposition 203: English language education for children in public schools.* Retrieved from http://apps.azsos.gov/election/2000/Info/pubpamphlet/english/prop203.htm

Athanases, S. Z., & de Oliveira, L. C. (2011). Toward program-wide coherence in preparing teachers to teach and advocate for English language learners. In T. Lucas (Ed.), *Teacher preparation for linguistically diverse classrooms: A resource for teacher educators* (pp. 195–215). New York, NY: Routledge.

Bilingual Education Act, Pub. L. No. (90-247), 81 Stat. 816 (1968).

Bransford, J., Darling-Hammond, L., & LePage, P. (2005). Introduction. In L. Darling-Hammond & J. Bransford (Eds.), *Preparing teachers for a chingking world: What teachers should learn and be able to do* (pp. 1–39). San Francisco, CA: Jossey-Bass.

Brown, H. D. (2007). *Principles of language learning and teaching* (5th ed.). White Plains, NY: Pearson/Longman.

Burke, A., & de Oliveira, L. C. (2012). Educational policies in the United States and implications for English learners. *Revista Brasileira de Linguistica Aplicada, 12*(2), 311–329.

California Secretary of State. (1998). *Proposition 227: English language in public schools.* Retrieved from http://primary98.sos.ca.gov/VoterGuide/Propositions/227.htm

Council for Accreditation of Counseling and Related Educational Programs. (2001). *CACREP accreditation manual.* Alexandria, VA: Author.

Council for Accreditation of Counseling and Related Educational Programs. (2009). CACREP standards. Retrieved from http://www.cacrep.org/wp-content/uploads /2013/12/2009-Standards.pdf

Council for Accreditation of Counseling and Related Educational Programs. (2015). 2016 CACREP standards. Retrieved from http://www.cacrep.org/about-cacrep /2016-cacrep-standards/

de Jong, E., & Harper, C. (2005). Preparing mainstream teachers for English language learners: Is being a good teacher good enough? *Teacher Education Quarterly, 32*(2), 101–124.

de Jong, E., & Harper, C. (2008). ESL is good teaching "plus": Preparing standard curriculum teachers for all learners. In M. E. Brisk (Ed.), *Language, culture, and community in teacher education* (pp. 127–148). New York, NY: Erlbaum.

Dotson-Blake, K. P., Foster, V., & Gressard, C. F. (2009). Ending the silence of the Mexican immigrant voice in public education: Creating culturally inclusive family-school-community partnerships. *Professional School Counseling, 12*(3), 230–239.

Faltis, C. (2006). *Teaching English language learners in elementary school communities: A joinfostering approach* (4th ed). Upper Saddle River, NJ: Pearson.

Fillmore, L. W., & Snow, C. (2005). What teachers need to know about language. In C. T. Adger, C. E. Snow, & D. Christian (Eds.), *What teachers need to know about language* (pp.7–54). Washington, DC, and McHenry, IL: Center for Applied Linguistics and Delta Systems.

Friend, M., & Cook, L. (1992). *Interactions: Communication skills for school professionals.* White Plains, NY: Longman.

Ginn, S. J. (1924). Vocational guidance in Boston public schools. *The Vocational Guidance Magazine, 3,* 3–7.

Gysbers, N. C., & Henderson, P. (2006). *Developing & managing your school guidance and counseling program* (4th ed.). Alexandria, VA: American Counseling Association.

Halliday, M. A. K. (1993). Towards a language-based theory of learning. *Linguistics and Education, 5*(2), 93–116.

Hamerdinger, S., & Karlin, B. (2003). Therapy using interpreters: Questions on the use of interpreters in therapeutic settings for monolingual therapists. *Journal of American Deafness and Rehabilitation Association, 36*(3), 12–30.

Holcomb-McCoy, C. (2004). Assessing the multicultural competence of school counselors: A checklist. *Professional School Counseling, 7*(3), 178–186.

Kramsch, C. (1998). *Language and culture.* Oxford, England: Oxford University Press.

Lau v. Nichols, 483 F.2d 791 (9th Cir. 1973); 414 U.S. 563 (1974).

Levy, M. (2007). Culture, culture learning and new technologies: Towards a pedagogical framework. *Language Learning & Technology, 11*(2), 104–127.

Lucas, T., & Villegas, A. M. (2010). The missing piece in teacher education: The preparation of linguistically responsive teachers. *National Society for the Study of Education, 109*(2), 297–318.

Lucas, T., & Villegas, A. M. (2011). A framework for preparing linguistically responsive teachers. In T. Lucas (Ed.), *Teacher preparation for linguistically diverse classrooms: A resource for teacher educators* (pp. 55–72). New York, NY: Routledge.

Lucas, T., Villegas, A. M., & Freedson-Gonzalez, M. (2008). Linguistically responsive teacher education: Preparing classroom teachers to teach English language learners. *Journal of Teacher Education, 59*(4), 361–373.

McCall-Perez, Z. (2000). The counselor as advocate for English language learners: An action research approach. *Professional School Counseling, 4*(1), 13–22.

Menken, K. (2008). *English learners left behind: Standardized testing as language policy.* Clevedon, United Kingdom: Multilingual Matters.

Menyuk, P., & Brisk, M. E. (2005). *Language development and education: Children with varying language experience.* New York, NY: Palgrave Macmillan.

Murray, D., & Christison, M. (2011). *What English language teachers need to know volume 1: Understanding learning.* New York, NY: Routledge.

Myers, G. E. (1923). A critical review of present developments in vocational guidance with special reference to future prospects. *The Vocational Guidance Magazine, 2,* 139–142.

National Clearinghouse for English Language Acquisition. (2006). *The growing numbers of limited English proficient students: 1993/94–2003/4.* Washington, DC: U.S. Department of Education, Office of English Language Acquisition.

The National Defense Education Act (NDEA) of 1958, Pub. L. No. 85-864 (1958).

No Child Left Behind Act of 2001, Pub. L. No. 107-110 (2002).

Paredes, M. A. B. (2010). *Addressing the professional development awareness needs of school counselors regarding English language learners (ELLs): Using the school cultural capital game to enhance level of self-efficacy with ELLs and attitudes toward immigrants* (Unpublished doctoral dissertation). University of North Carolina, Greensboro.

Parsons, F. (1909). *Choosing a vocation.* Boston, MA: Houghton Mifflin.

Pederson, P. (1999). *Multiculturalism as a fourth fource.* Philadelphia, PA: Bruner/Mazel.

Pereira, N., & de Oliveira, L. C. (2015). Meeting the linguistic needs of gifted English language learners: What teachers need to know. *Teaching Exceptional Children, 47*(1), 208–215.

Ratts, M. J., Singh, A. A., Nassar-McMillan, S., Butler, S. K., & McCullough, J. R. (2015). *Multicultural and Social Justice Counseling Competencies.* Retrieved from http:// www.multiculturalcounseling.org/index.php?option=com_content&view=article&id =205:amcd-endorses-multicultural-and-social-justice-counseling-competencies&catid =1:latest&Itemid=123

Ravitch, S. M. (2006). *School counseling principles: Multiculturalism and diversity.* Alexandria, VA: American School Counselor Association Press.

Robinson, T. L. (1999). The intersection of dominant discourses across race, gender, and other identities. *Journal of Counseling & Development, 77,* 73–79.

Schleppegrell, M. J. (2004). *The language of schooling: A functional linguistic perspective.* Mahwah, NJ: Lawrence Erlbaum Associates.

Secretary of the Commonwealth. (2002). *The official Massachusetts information for voters: The 2002 ballot questions.* Retrieved from http://www.sec.state.ma.us/ele/elepdf /ifv02.pdf

Selinker, L. (1972). Interlanguage. *International Review of Applied Linguistics, 10,* 201–231.

Teachers of English to Speakers of Other Languages. (2006). *PreK–12 English language proficiency standards.* Alexandria, VA: Author.

Téllez, K., & Waxman, H. C. (Eds.). (2006). *Preparing quality educators for English language learners: Research, policies, and practices.* Mahwah, NJ: Lawrence Erlbaum Associates.

Title III Language Instruction for Limited English Proficient and Immigrant Students. Public Law 107-110 (2002).

Title VII of the Elementary and Secondary Education Act of 1965. Public Law 90-247 (1968).

Tyler, L. E. (1960). *The vocational defense counseling and guidance training institutes program: A report of the first 50 institutes.* Washington, DC: U.S. Department of Health, Education, and Welfare, Office of Education.

Villegas, A. M., & Lucas, T. (2007). The culturally responsive teacher. *Educational Leadership, 64*(6), 28–33.

Wrenn, C. G. (1962). *The counselor in a changing world.* Washington, DC: American Personnel and Guidance Association.

Appendix A: Resources for Professional Development

Following are some websites, publications, and other resources for working with ELLs.

Websites

- "School Counselors and School Psychologists: Collaborating to Ensure Minority Students Receive Appropriate Consideration for Special Educational Programs" (Reading Rockets): http://www.readingrockets.org/article/school-counselors-and-school -psychologists-collaborating-ensure-minority-students-receive

- "The Guidance Counselor's Role in Ensuring Equal Educational Opportunity" (U.S. Department of Education): http://www2.ed.gov/about/offices/list/ocr/docs/hq43ef.html

- Web Resources for Guidance Counselors (Colorín Colorado): http://www.colorincolorado.org/web_resources/by_audience /guidance_counselors/
  Resources for Guidance Counselors (United Federation of Teachers): http://www.uft.org/chapters/guidance-counselors/resources

Publications

Bemak, F., & Chung, R. C. (2005). Advocacy as a critical role for urban school counselors: Working toward equity and social justice. *Professional School Counseling, 8*, 196–202.

Burkard, A. W., Martinez, M. J., & Holtz, C. A. (2009). Closing the achievement gap: School counselors' social justice imperative. In J. G. Ponterotto, J. M. Casas, L. Suzuki, & C. M. Alexander (Eds.), *Handbook of multicultural counseling.* New York, NY: Sage.

Burnham, J. J., Mantero, M., & Hooper, L. M. (2009). Experiential training: Connecting school counselors-in-training, English as a second language (ESL) teachers and ESL students. *Journal of Multicultural Counseling and Development, 37*(1), 2–14.

Goh, M., Wahl, K. H., McDonald, J. K., Brissett, A. A., & Yoon, E. (2007). Working with immigrant students in schools: The role of school counselors in building cross-cultural bridges. *Journal of Multicultural Counseling and Development, 35,* 66–79.

Hagan, M. (2004). Acculturation and an ESL program: A service-learning project. *Journal of Multicultural Counseling and Development, 32,* 443–448.

Holcomb-McCoy, C. (2004). Assessing the multicultural competence of school counselors: A checklist. *Professional School Counseling, 7*(3), 178–186.

Malott, K. M., Paone, T. R., Humphreys, K., & Martinez, T. (2010). Use of group counseling to address ethnic identity development: Application of adolescents of Mexican descent. *Professional School Counseling, 13,* 257–267.

McCall-Perez, Z. (2000). The counselor as advocate for English language learners: An action research approach. *Professional School Counseling, 4*(1), 13–23.

Park-Taylor, J., Walsh, M., & Ventura, A. B. (2007). Creating healthy acculturation pathways: Integrating theory and research to inform counselors' work with immigrant children. *Professional School Counseling, 11*(1), 25–34.

Ravitch, S. M. (2006). *School counseling principles: Multiculturalism and diversity.* Alexandria, VA: American School Counselor Association Press.

Roysircar, G., Gard, G., Hubbell, R., & Ortega, M. (2005). Development of counseling trainees' multicultural awareness through mentoring English as a second language students. *Journal of Multicultural Counseling and Development, 33,* 17–36.

Santos de Barona, M., & Barona, A. (2006). School counselors and school psychologists collaborating to ensure minority students receive appropriate consideration for special education programs. *Professional School Counseling, 10,* 3–13.

Shi, Q., & Steen, S. (2010). Group work with English as second language (ESL) students: Integrating academic and behavior considerations. *Journal of School Counseling, 8*(41), 41.

Spomer, M. L., & Cowen, E. L. (2001). A comparison of the school mental health referrals profile of young ESL and English speaking children. *Journal of Community Psychology, 29*(1), 69–82.

Williams, F. C., & Butler, S. K. (2003). Concerns of newly arrived immigrant students: Implications for school counselors. *Professional School Counseling, 7*(1), 9–14.